Contents

Introduction ....

Definitions (arranged

Agency Responses

Law

Key Factors Supporting Effective Child Protection

Protection in Specific Circumstances

Best Practice

In exercising social services functions, local authorities are required to act under the general guidance of the Secretary of State(s.7(1)Local Authority Social Services Act 1970). In R v Islington LBC, ex parte Ritson (1996) 32 BMLR 136 at 140 Sedley J described the effect of s.7(1):'in my view Parliament, by s.7(1), has required local authorities to follow the path charted by the Secretary of State's guidance, with liberty to deviate from it where the local authority judges , on admissible grounds, that there is good reason to do so, but without freedom to take a substantially different course'.

This direction has since been followed in R v Lambeth LBC ex p K [2000] 3 CCLR 141 and in R (on the application of AB and SB) v Nottingham City Council [2001] 3 FCR 350

The text of this guide reflects statutory and the most significant case law as at March2003

Abbreviations

ACA = Adoption and Children Act 2002

CA 1989 = Children Act 1989

CDA 1998 = Crime and Disorder Act 1998

CJCA 2000 = Criminal Justice and Courts Act 2000

EA 2002 = Education Act 2002

FLA 1996 = Family Law Act 1996

FLR = Family Law Reports

FLRA 1969 = Family Law Reform Act 1969

FLRA 1987 = Family Law Reform Act 1987

MHA 1983 = Mental Health Act 1983

PHA 1997 = Protection From Harassment Act 1997

POCA 1999 = Protection of Children Act 1999

SOA 1997 = Sex Offenders Act 1997

Introduction

- This guide is for those in England and Wales who provide, or support providers of, child protection services.

- It is designed for rapid reference by:

    - Doctors, nurses and other health professionals

    - Social workers

    - Police and probation officers

    - Education staff

    - Others in statutory and independent settings who suspect a child is being abused or neglected

- The guide provides a simple, accurate summary and reinforces understanding of current law and government guidance.

- The guide should be used only to supplement, not replace information derived from the above sources or from local guidance, procedures and legal advice.

- Appendix 1 summarises current law concerning consent and refusal by children of assessment or treatment.

- Appendix 2 offers a summary of the current requirements and professional expectations of doctors with respect to confidentiality and contraception for those aged less than 16 years old.

Definitions [arranged alphabetically]

Care Plan [s.31A CA 1989 as inserted by s.121 ACA 2002]

- Where an application is made which might result in a Care Order, the appropriate local authority (the one proposed to be designated in the order) must, within a time-scale directed by the court prepare a 'care plan' (referred to in ACA 2002 as a 's.31A plan') for the future care of the child.

- While the application is pending, the local authority must keep the plan under review and revise or replace it if this is required.

NB. A care plan must give any prescribed information and do so in the prescribed manner.

Child [s.105(1) CA 1989].

- For the purposes of child protection, a 'child' is a person of less than 18 years of age.

'Child in Need' [s.17(10);(11) CA 1989]

- A child is 'in need' if:

    - S/he is unlikely to achieve or maintain, or have the opportunity to so do, a reasonable standard of health or development without provision of services by a local authority, or if

- Her/his health or development is likely to be significantly impaired, or further impaired, without such services, or

- S/he is disabled

NB. Health = physical or mental; Development = physical, intellectual, emotional, social or behavioural; Disabled = blind, deaf, dumb or suffering from mental disorder of any kind or substantially and permanently handicapped by illness, injury or congenital deformity, or other such disability as may be prescribed.

■ Each local authority has a general duty to safeguard and promote welfare of children in need its area, and so far as is consistent with that duty, promote their upbringing by their families by providing a range and level of services appropriate to their needs [s.17 (1)CA 1989].

NB. A child who is at risk of 'significant harm' (see below) may be assumed to be a child in need and therefore eligible for family support services.

■ Such children may now include children in Young Offender Institutions and in young persons' wings of prisons following the decision in R on the application of the Howard League for Penal Reform v The Secretary of State for the Home Office (judgement issued 29 November 2002) and requires an amendment of para. 3.1.4 of PSO 4950 which wrongly stated the Children Act 1989 did not apply to children in prison establishments.

Child Protection Plan

- The 'core group' (see below) is responsible for developing the 'outline child protection plan' agreed at an initial conference into a 'child protection plan' which:

  - Identifies risks and means of protection

  - Takes account of issues of ethnicity, culture, parental wishes (insofar as these are consistent with child's welfare) and any special needs

  - Describes needs and required services and establishes objectives including time-scales

  - Agrees short and longer term actions to promote child's health and development and

  - Allocates clear tasks (and contact schedules) for professionals and family members

  - Determines a contingency plan to deal with insufficient progress or changed circumstances

Child Protection Register

- A list of all children resident in the social services area (including any placed there by another local authority) who are considered to be at continuing risk of significant harm, and for whom there is a child protection plan.

- The main purpose of the register is to make relevant agencies and individuals aware of those children assessed to be at continuing risk of significant harm.

- Police and health professionals must be able to access the register in and out of office hours.

Core Assessment [Para.3.11Framework for the Assessment of Children in Need & Their Families]

- An in-depth assessment which addresses the central or most important aspects of the needs of a child and the capacity of her/his parents or caregivers to respond appropriately to those needs within the wider family and community context.

NB.   Though led by social services, such assessments (which must completed within 35 working days) will invariably involve other agencies or independent professionals).

Core Group

- The core group is responsible for developing the outline protection plan into a full child protection plan.

- Membership should include the key worker who leads the core group, the child if appropriate, family members and professionals / foster carers who will have direct contact with the family.

- The first meeting of the core group should take place within 10 working days of an initial protection conference.

Emotional Abuse

- Emotional abuse is the persistent emotional ill treatment of a child such as to cause severe and persistent effects on the child's emotional development.

- It may involve conveying to children that they are worthless or unloved, inadequate, or valued only insofar as they meet the needs of another person. It may involve causing children to feel frightened or in danger or feature developmentally inappropriate expectations.

- Some level of emotional abuse is involved in all types of ill treatment of children, though emotional abuse may occur alone.

- Where this form of abuse is suspected, advice should be sought from those with expertise in child or adolescent mental health.

Key Worker

- The key worker (a qualified social worker from social services or NSPCC) is responsible for making sure that the outline child protection plan is developed into a more detailed inter-agency plan and has the lead role in inter-agency work with the family.

- S/he should complete the core assessment of child / family securing contributions from core group members and other as necessary and review progress against the agreed objectives.

Local Authority (LA) [s.105 CA 1989]

- Means a County Council, Metropolitan District, London Borough or Unitary Authority, not just social services.

'Looked After' Child [s.22 CA 1989]

- Children 'looked after' by a local authority may be 'accommodated', 'in care' or 'remanded / detained'.

- Accommodation is a voluntary arrangement in which the local authority does not gain parental responsibility and no notice is required for removal of the child.

- 'In care' means that a court has made a child subject of a Care Order which gives the local authority parental responsibility and (some) authority to limit parents' exercise of their continuing parental responsibility.

- A local authority is authorised to detain those in the third category who may acquire such status as a result of:

  - Remand by a court following criminal charges

  - Detention following arrest by police

  - An Emergency Protection Order (which also awards temporary parental responsibility to the local authority) or Child Assessment Order

  - A 'criminal' Supervision Order with a residence requirement.

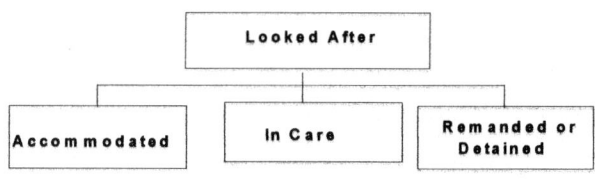

Neglect

- Neglect is the persistent failure to meet a child's basic physical and/or psychological needs, likely to result in the serious impairment of her/his health and development, including non-organic failure to thrive.

- Neglect may involve parental failure to provide adequate food, shelter or clothing, protection from physical harm or danger or ensure access to appropriate medical care / treatment (may also include neglect of child's basic emotional needs).

- Evidence of neglect is built up over time and can cover a range of parenting tasks. Typical features include:

  - Failure by parents or carers to meet the basic essential needs e.g. adequate food, clothes, warmth, hygiene and medical care

  - A child seen to be listless, apathetic and unresponsive with no apparent medical cause

  - Failure of a child to grow within normal expected pattern, with accompanying pallor and weight loss

- Observed thriving of child away from the home environment
- Voracious appetite

Outline Child Protection Plan

- Following a decision made at an initial or review conference to register or continue registration, an outline child protection plan should detail conference recommendations and include:

  - Broad objectives for the child's welfare
  - Identification of risk and protective factors
  - Types of services required including which agencies or individuals (including family members) are accountable for their provision
  - Required outcomes
  - A contingency plan

Paramountcy Principle [s.1(1) CA 1989]

- When a court determines any question with respect to a child's upbringing, administration of property or income, the child's welfare must be the paramount consideration.

- The House of Lords has confirmed that where both parent and child are 'children' within the meaning of the Act, the needs of the younger (non-parent) child are paramount [Birmingham City Council v H (No.2) 1 FLR 883 1993].

Parental Responsibility [s.3 CA 1989]

- 'Parental responsibility' means all the rights, duties, powers, responsibilities and authority which by law a parent has in relation to a child and her/his property.

- Where a child's parents were married to each other at any time following her/his conception they each have parental responsibility for the child [s.2(1) CA 1989 & s.1 FLRA 1987].

- Parental responsibility can be lost only if a child is freed for adoption, adopted, attains the age of 18 or dies.

- Each parent / other person with parental responsibility can act independently in the exercise of it e.g. giving consent to medical treatment.

- If a married couple separate or divorce, they both continue to have parental responsibility for their child/ren.

- Where a child's mother and father were not married to each other at any time following her/his conception:

  - The mother has parental responsibility for the child

  - The father does not have it unless he acquires it in accordance with the provisions of the Children Act 1989 [s.2(2) CA 1989]

- An unmarried father may obtain parental responsibility for his child as a result of:

- A formal 'Parental Responsibility Agreement' drawn up in a prescribed form with the child's mother and lodged in the Principal Registry of the High Court's Family Division [s.4(1)(b) CA 1989]

- An application to a court for a 'Parental Responsibility Order' [s.4(1)(a) ibid]

- A Residence Order being made in his favour in which case a Parental Responsibility Order must also be made under s.4 [s.12(1) ibid]

- The death of the child's mother (if she had nominated him as guardian for their child in a will [s.5(5)] ibid)

- A court's direction that on the death of all those already holding parental responsibility he should become child's guardian [s.5(6) ibid]

NB. *The Adoption and Children Act 2002 contains provisions changing the allocation and acquisition of parental responsibility by birth fathers, step fathers and special guardians though these are unlikely to be implemented immediately.*

- ■ The essence of parental responsibility is that it is a status not merely a set of rights, duties and powers [Re S (Parental Responsibility) [1995] 2 FLR 648].

- ■ Nonetheless, the practical advantages of such a status include:

  - A right to receive educational reports and provide consent to school trips

- A right to consent to treatment for, and receive medical reports about the child

- An ability to sign official papers e.g. passport application

- An ability to prevent a child's mother removing her/him from the UK

- A right to object to a proposed change of name

- A right to object to a child being accommodated by a local authority and an ability to lawfully remove her/him

- Being regarded as a 'parent' for purposes of adoption proceedings

NB. *In order to comply with Article 8(1) of the European Convention, best practice is to treat the unmarried father who does not have parental responsibility as possessing full rights. [see companion guide to Children Act 1989 in the Context of the Human Rights Act 1998 for comprehensive coverage of the significance of the European Convention for work with children and families].*

Physical Abuse

- Actual or likely physical injury to a child where there is evidence or reason to suspect the injury or likely injury was deliberately inflicted or not prevented.

- Physical abuse may involve hitting, shaking, throwing, poisoning, burning or scalding, drowning, suffocating or otherwise causing physical harm to a child.

- Physical harm may also be caused when a parent or carer feigns symptoms of, or deliberately causes, ill-health to a child (variously described as 'fabricated or induced illness' or 'Munchausen's syndrome by proxy').

NB. See 'Safeguarding Children in Whom Illness is Fabricated or Induced' DH 2002 www.doh.gov.uk/qualityprotects which provides information supplementary to Working Together to Safeguard Children DH 1999 / Welsh Assembly 2000.

Sexual Abuse

- Sexual abuse is defined as the sexual exploitation of children (under 18 years old) and involves forcing or enticing a child to take part in sexual activities, whether or not s/he is aware of what is happening.

- Activities may involve physical contact, including penetrative (e.g. rape and buggery) and other non-penetrative acts.

- Sexual abuse may take non-physical forms e.g. involving a child in looking at, or in production of pornography, watching sexual activities or encouraging her/him to behave in sexually inappropriate ways.

- For the purpose of criminal prosecution, sexual abuse will be related to the legal age of consent.

NB. See supplement to Working Together entitled Safeguarding Children involved in Prostitution (DH May 2000 www.doh.gov.uk/quality)

Sex Offender Register

- The Sex Offenders Act 1997 introduced a requirement for those cautioned or convicted of specified categories of sexual offences to inform the police of their name and address, and update them about any changes thereof.

- The police service is responsible for maintaining the register of relevant offenders.

- Police and probation services are responsible under the Criminal Justice Act 2000 for general multi-agency public protection arrangements (MAPPA) and for convening multi-agency public protection panels (MAPPPs) where practical strategies to assess and reduce the risk posed by targeted individuals can be developed.

Significant Harm [s.31 CA 1989]

- 'Significant harm' is the threshold which justifies compulsory intervention in family life.

- Harm means ill-treatment or impairment of health or development (to include impairment suffered from seeing or hearing ill-treatment of another introduced by s.117 ACA 2002).

- Development means physical, intellectual, emotional, social or behavioural development and health means physical or mental health. Ill-treatment includes sexual abuse and forms of ill-treatment which are not physical.

- Where the question of whether harm suffered by a child is significant turns on the child's health and development, her/his health or development must be compared with that which could reasonably be expected of a similar child [s.31(10) CA 1989].

NB. *The definition of 'harm' in s.31(9) CA 1989 will be extended by the ACA 2002 to include 'for example, impairment suffered from seeing or hearing the ill-treatment of another [s.120 ACA 2002].*

Welfare Checklist [s.1 (3) CA 1989]

- In considering an opposed s.8 Order or Care or Supervision Order (including Interim Care and Supervision and Education Supervision Orders), the court must have regard to checklist of:

  - Child's wishes / feelings

  - Physical, emotional, educational needs

  - Likely effect of change of circumstances

  - Age, sex, background, relevant characteristics (this should include race, culture, religion and language)

  - Actual or potential harm

  - Capability of parents / relevant others to meet child's needs

  - Available range of powers

Social Services

- A key objective for social services is to ensure that children are protected from significant harm.

- Specific responsibilities include:

  - Undertaking, in conjunction with the police, enquiries under s.47 Children Act 1989 wherever there is reasonable cause to suspect that a child is suffering or is likely to suffer abuse or neglect

  - Convening and chairing child protection conferences

  - Maintaining the child protection register

  - Providing a key worker for every child on the protection register

  - Ensuring that the agencies who are party to the protection plan co-ordinate their activities to protect the child

  - Undertaking a core assessment in relation to each child on the register, ensuring that other agencies contribute as necessary to the assessment

  - Convening regular reviews of the child's progress through both core group and child protection conference review meetings

Police

- Protecting life and preventing crime are primary tasks of the police and provide the rationale for investigating and taking action with respect to criminal offences against children.

- Child Protection Units (CPUs) usually take primary responsibility for investigating child abuse cases within families or committed by a carer (local criminal investigation division (CID) officers deal with cases which fall outside the CPU's remit).

- The CPU role is generally to investigate possible offences which occur:

  - Within the nuclear or extended family

  - In respect of a looked after child, where the alleged abuser is the carer or an employee of the organisation

  - Where the person in question is an adult now m but abuse allegedly occurred when s/he was a child in either of the above circumstances

NB. The Metropolitan Police Service has extended the remit of its CPUs to cover abuse by those known to a child and by strangers.

- 'Police Powers of Protection' (see p.44) put police services in a special position since they do not have to apply to court first to use it.

NB. *The 'Safeguarding Children' report October 2002*
included a recommendation that police services
should review and clarify the role, remit, location and
status of child protection units to ensure all abuse of
children is dealt with to a consistently high standard.

Other responsibilities and recommendations for
police and/or Home Office are identified in Lord
Laming's report (recommendations 91 –108).

Health Services

- All health staff have a vital contribution to child
  protection through their:

  - Recognition of children in need of support

  - Participation in enquiries about the needs of an
    individual child

  - Assessment of a child's needs and her/his
    parents' capacity to meet them

  - Planning and provision of support to children in
    need

  - Participation in case conferences / reviews

  - Planning and participation in protection plans to
    support a child at risk

  - Provision of therapeutic help to a family .g.
    Child and Adolescent Mental Health Services

- Each Primary Care Trust (PCT) is responsible for identifying a 'designated' senior paediatrician and senior nurse to take a professional lead on all aspects of the health services' contribution to child protection.

- Provider Trusts are responsible for identifying 'named' doctor/s and nurse/s for child protection who are responsible within their organisation for ensuring:

  - Provision of expert health advice on child protection to staff and other agencies, as appropriate, regarding individual cases and a contribution to planning of services

  - Provision of inputs to ACPC agencies in the ongoing development of London-wide policies, procedures and guidance

  - Identification of training needs of all staff, including the training needs of GPs and all medical personnel

  - Multi-disciplinary training

  - The review of child protection practice and the setting of standards in their trust

  - Systems between different parts of the health services for the transfer of children's records and any other relevant information

  - Service level agreements that incorporate child protection requirements including clear monitoring processes

- Effective systems of child protection audit to monitor the application of agreed child protection standards

- Appropriate doctors / nurses nomination to undertake the trust's responsibility for case reviews

- Dissemination of recommendations and implications of case reviews in conjunction with the chief executives concerned

- Identification and reporting of unmet needs in service provision to senior managers and the consequences of the situation

- Co-ordination and liaison with other professionals with child protection responsibilities within health services and other partner agencies

- General Practitioners (GPs) have a critical role in the prevention, initial identification and management of child abuse and neglect. GPs are responsible for ensuring that their own staff as well as any commissioned to provide services comply with locally agreed procedures.

NB.   Recommendations 64-90 inclusive of Lord Laming's report offer elaboration.

Education Services

Local Education Authority (LEA)

- New duties are imposed by s.175 EA 2002 e.g. s.175(1) - 'A LEA shall make arrangements for ensuring that the functions conferred upon them in their capacity as a LEA are exercised with a view to safeguarding and promoting the welfare of children'.

- The LEA must nominate a lead officer responsible for co-ordinating policy and action on child protection across schools maintained by the authority and for providing advice to them (*Circular 10/95*).

- LEAs must ensure all staff in maintained and non-maintained sectors are aware of child protection procedures.

- LEAs must keep up to date lists of designated staff and ensure that these staff receive appropriate training and support (see below).

Schools & Colleges

- Through their daily contact with children, teachers and other staff in maintained, grant maintained and independent schools, sixth form and further education colleges are well placed to observe signs of abuse, changes in behaviour or a failure to develop.

- Schools must contribute to child protection through the:
  - Provision of a safe environment for children
  - Use of the curriculum to understand what is and is not acceptable behaviour and how to speak up regarding their concerns
  - Recognition of significant harm and referral to social services
- All schools must have policies and procedures which reflect the roles of staff and parents regarding:
  - Child protection
  - The use of force to control or restrain pupils
  - Identification and response to bullying
  - Identification and response to racism
- The 'designated' member of staff is responsible for:
  - Arranging training for colleagues
  - Producing internal procedures to be followed by all staff in the establishment when concerns arise
  - Keeping all staff (including secretarial, midday supervisors, caretakers, school helpers etc) updated with current procedures, ensuring new and temporary staff are familiar with protection responsibilities
  - Provision of advice and support to staff
  - Referring any concerns as soon as they arise to social services

- Monitoring attendance and development of children whose names are currently on the child protection register and informing the social services of proposed or actual change of school

- Ensuring all relevant information about a child is disseminated to appropriate school staff

- Ensuring that complete records are sent on to the receiving school, whether a child changes as a natural progression or for any other reason

Schools Governors & Governing Bodies

- S.175(2) EA 2002 states that the governing body of a maintained school shall make arrangements for ensuring their functions relating to conduct of the school are exercised with a view to safeguarding and promoting the welfare of pupils at the school.

- S.175(3) states the governing body of an institution within the further education sector shall make arrangements for ensuring that their functions relating to the conduct of the institution are exercised with a view to safeguarding and promoting the welfare of children receiving education or training at the institution.

NB. *S175(4) EA 2002 states that 'an authority or body mentioned in any of subsections 1-3 shall, in considering what arrangements are required to be made by them under that subsection, have regard to any guidance given from time to time in relation to England by the Secretary of State or in relation to Wales by the National Assembly for Wales.*

S.175 (5) states that in this section 'child means a person under the age of 18; governing body in relation to an institution within the further education sector has the meaning given by s.90 Further and Higher Education Act 1992; maintained school means a community foundation or voluntary school, a community or foundation special school or a maintained nursery school.

- Governing bodies and proprietors of non-maintained establishments must then ensure that appropriate child protection procedures are in place, seeking advice as necessary from the LEA or social services.

- School governors have a specific contribution to make if allegations are made against a head teacher.

Investigation & Referral Support Co-ordinators

- 'Investigation and referral support co-ordinator' posts have been established by the DfES, each responsible for working with and supporting a cluster of LEAs.

- The post-holders play a key role in providing strategic advice and support to the education sector in areas of child protection policy, practice and training including the monitoring of systems that protect children and young people whilst supporting staff.

- Co-ordinators aim to:

- Ensure that allegations against teachers and other staff are expedited and that staff suspensions are for the minimum time period

- Support and strengthen all schools' roles in identifying children at risk, ensuring where necessary, social services and police intervention

- Improve the support and guidance available to all head teachers, governors and LEAs

Education Welfare Officers

- In their direct welfare work with families, EWOs may recognise child protection issues and must refer these to social services.

- EWOs should assist the designated teacher in monitoring children whose names appear on the child protection register.

- EWOs are able to provide advice and support to other education staff on child protection matters.

Other Agencies

- The following agencies also have a direct contribution with respect to prevention or reporting, as well as a supportive role in investigation of abuse and neglect:

  - Housing Authorities
  - Children and Family Courts Advisory and Support Service
  - Probation
  - Youth Justice & Prison Services
  - Armed Services
  - NSPCC
  - Early Years Development & Child Care Partnerships
  - Faith groups / churches
  - Ambulance & Fire & Rescue Services
  - Connexions
  - Ofsted
  - National Care Standards Commission
  - Immigration & Nationality Department
  - Youth, Cultural, Library & Leisure Services
  - All other organisations which deal with children

*NB. 'Safeguarding Children' and Lord Laming's reports both reinforce the responsibility of **all** agencies to work together to protect children.*

- The support of the wider community should also be encouraged by means of:

  - Open communication with local people and media about agencies' work

  - Provision of accessible information and advice in a form which is clear and relevant to all

  - Publicising and promoting how and when to make contact where concerns about a child exist and what response to expect

  - Offering advice and training to community, religious and other voluntary groups on how to provide a safe service to children

Area Child Protection Committee (ACPC)

- Each ACPC must include the main agencies and professional groups responsible for helping to protect children from abuse and neglect.

Aims & Objectives

- Overall aims are to ensure effective collaboration of all agencies to protect from abuse, neglect and consequent significant harm and thus bring about positive outcomes for, children in the local authority area.

- Specific objectives are to:

  - Develop and agree inter-agency policies and procedures consistent with *Working Together to Safeguard Children*

  - Audit and evaluate how well local services are working together

  - Put in place performance objectives and indicators for child protection in the context of local Children's Services Plans

  - Encourage and develop effective working relationships between different services and professional groups

  - Ensure agreement and understanding across agencies about operational definitions and thresholds for intervention

- Apply lessons learnt from national and local research and experience

- Undertake appropriate case reviews and ensure lessons are understood and acted upon

- Specify and ensure delivery of effective inter-agency training

- Raise community awareness of need to safeguard and contribute to children's welfare

■ The ACPC must address the needs of children:

- Abused and neglected within families including those affected as a result of domestic violence

- Abused outside of the family either by adults known or unknown to them

- Abused or neglected by professional carers whilst in institutional care and/or living from away from home

- Abused by other children

- Abused through prostitution

- Who misuse drugs and alcohol and

- Who perpetrate abuse

NB. *ACPCs need to address the implications of R on the application of the Howard League for Penal Reform v The Secretary of State for the Home Office (see p.3) which wrongly stated the Children Act 1989 did not apply to children in prison establishments.*

- Social services has lead responsibility for establishment and effective working of each ACPC though all constituent agencies are responsible for contributing fully and effectively to its effective operation.

Membership & Structure

- ACPC members must be senior managers able to commit their agency to agreed policy and include:

  - Social services and the local education authority

  - Health services, including managerial and professional expertise and responsibilities

  - Police

  - Probation

  - NSPCC (when active in the area)

  - Domestic violence forum

  - Armed services (where there is a significant presence in the area)

- The ACPC must be chaired by an individual who can command the respect and support of member agencies and who has a firm grasp of local operational issues.

- Chairing may be rotated between agencies or be undertaken by a person who is independent of all agencies.

- ACPCs have discretion to set up and maintain short-term or ongoing sub-groups / committees, e.g:

  - Policy and Practice

  - Audit and Management Information

  - Serious Case Review

  - Training, Public Relations and Communication

- Each ACPC should produce an annual business plan setting out a work programme for forthcoming year including measurable objectives and relevant management information on protection activity and progress on declared objectives in previous 12 months.

Chapter 8 / Serious Case Review

- The ACPC should always commission a serious case review (as described in chapter 8 of *Working Together to Safeguard Children*) when a child dies (including suicide) and abuse or neglect is known or suspected to be a factor.

- Such a review should also be considered when concerns exist about the way in which local professionals and services worked together for a child who:

  - Sustained a potentially life threatening injury through abuse or neglect

  - Experienced serious sexual abuse or

- Sustained serious and permanent impairment of health or development as result of abuse or neglect

■ The purpose of such a review is to:

- Establish whether there are lessons to be learnt about the way in which local professionals and agencies work together

- Implement any required changes so as to better protect children in the future

■ The processes involved in initiating, conducting and reporting upon a serious case review are described in *Working Together to Safeguard Children*

NB. *'Learning from Past Experience' DH 2002 provides a review of 40 Serious Case Reviews completed in recent years [www.doh.gov.uk/qualityprotects].*

Primary Legislation

- The main sources of English primary legislation relating to the care and protection of children are:

  - Children Act 1989 (as amended by Adoption and Children Act 2002)

  - Part IV Family Law Act 1996

  - Protection From Harassment Act 1997

  - Sex Offenders Act 1997

  - Protection of Children Act 1999

  - Provisions of Criminal Justice Act 1991 (as amended) relating to use of video recording in criminal proceedings

- In discharging any of their responsibilities, including child protection the Human Rights Act 1998 [s.6] now requires all 'public authorities' e.g. social services, health trusts, police, courts etc, to act toward children and adults in ways which are compatible with the European Convention on Human Rights with respect to:

  - Article 2   Respect to Life

  - Article 3   Prohibition of Torture

  - Article 4   Prohibition of Slavery and Forced Labour

  - Article 5   Right to Liberty and Security

  - Article 6   Right to a Fair Trial

- Article 7   No Punishment Without Law
- Article 8   Right to Respect for Private and Family Life
- Article 9   Freedom of Thought, Conscience and Religion
- Article 10   Freedom of Expression
- Article 11   Freedom of Assembly and Association
- Article 12   Right to Marry

■ Article 14 of the Convention provides that the enjoyment of the above rights must be allowed without discrimination on any ground such as sex, race, colour, language, religion, political or other opinion, national or social origin, association with a national minority, property, birth or other status.

■ A key concept of the Convention of particular relevance to child protection work is that of 'proportionality' i.e. any interference with a person's rights must be sanctioned by law, go no further than necessary and be proportionate to meet a 'pressing social need'.

■ For example, with respect to Article 8 – Respect for Private and Family Life, public authorities can override the right if it is necessary for 'public safety, to prevent crime, to protect health or morals or for the protection of the rights and freedoms of others'.

Inter Agency Co-operation [s.27 CA 1989]

- There is a mutual obligation on local authorities to assist one another unless this is in conflict with their own statutory duties.

Prevention of Neglect and Abuse [Sch.2 Para. 4 CA 1989]

- Each local authority must take reasonable steps through provision of family support services to prevent children within its area suffering ill treatment or neglect.

- The local authority must inform any other local authority if a child likely to suffer harm lives, or proposes to live in its area.

Local Authority Duty to Make Enquiries [s.47(1)(a) (i) – (iii) (b) CA 1989 as amended by CDA 1998]

- When told a child is subject of an Emergency Protection Order, Police Powers of Protection (see below), or the local authority has reasonable cause to **suspect** s/he is suffering / likely to suffer 'significant harm', or has contravened a ban imposed under the Crime and Disorder Act 1998, it must make enquiries to enable a decision on any necessary action to safeguard and promote the child's welfare.

NB. *The fact it need only be reasonable cause to **suspect** rather than **believe** was emphasised in R (On the Application of S) v Swindon BC & Another [2001] 3 FCR 702. Curfew contravention enquiries must be begun as soon as practicable and in any case within 48 hours of receiving information [s.47(1)(a)(iii) CA 1989 inserted by s.15(4) CDA 1998].*

- It is the duty of any local authority, education, housing or health trust, and the NSPCC (unless unreasonable to do so) to assist these enquiries e.g. provision of relevant information and advice [s.47 (9); (11) CA 1989].

- In Z v the UK [2001] 2 FLR 612(Formerly X v Bedfordshire CC) (HL), the European Court , ruled that failure by Bedfordshire County Council over 4 years to respond appropriately to concerns about four children who were victims of abuse and neglect by their parents, disclosed a breach of their human rights under Articles 3 (Freedom From Degrading Or Inhuman Treatment), and Article 13 (No Access To An Effective Remedy).

Provision of Accommodation to Protect Child [Sch.2 Para.5 CA 1989]

- If it appears to a local authority that a child living on particular premises is suffering or is likely to suffer ill treatment at the hands of another person living there, and that other person proposes to move out, the local authority may assist her/him to obtain alternative accommodation.

Emergency Protection Order (EPO) [s.44 CA 1989]

Applications

- By anyone without notice to the other parties, to a court or an individual magistrate.

NB.   It has been argued in Scotland that such applications being made without notice are in breach of Article 6 (Right To A Fair Trial). Reference might also be made the 'proportionality principle' [see above].

Grounds

- Court must be satisfied that:

  - There is reasonable cause to believe child is likely to suffer 'significant harm' if not removed to accommodation provided by applicant or does not remain in current location e.g. hospital [s.44 (1) (a) CA 1989] or

  - Local authority or NSPCC enquiry is at risk of being frustrated by unreasonable refusal of access [s.44 (1) (b) or (c) respectively ibid].

NB.   Social worker or NSPCC officer must produce identification. Early morning removal of a child is only justified where clear grounds exist that significant harm would otherwise occur or where vital evidence is obtainable only by such means [Re A (Minors) [1992] 1 All ER 153]and is proportionate to

*the end sought to be achieved (i.e. protection of the
health of children – Articles 8(1) & (2) of the
Convention). For the meaning of reasonable cause to
suspect here and in s 47 see R on the app of S v
Swindon Borough Council [2001] 3 FCR 702.*

Effect

- Gives applicant parental responsibility and right to
  remove / prevent removal of child.

- If, during the course of an EPO it appears to the
  applicant that it would be safe to return the child / allow
  her / him to leave the place in which s/he has been
  detained, the applicant must do this.

- If the child is returned home and it proves necessary
  (within the time limit of the EPO) the order can be
  reactivated.

Duration [s.45]

- Up to 8 days with one possible extension up to a further
  7 days.

- If the last day of an 8 day order falls on a public holiday
  (Christmas, Good Friday, a Bank Holiday or Sunday) the
  court may specify a period which ends at noon on the
  first later day which is not a public holiday.

*NB.   Court will consider appointment of a children's
       guardian at the application stage.*

Exclusion Requirements In Emergency Protection Orders [s.44A CA 1989 as inserted by s.52 & Sch.6 FLA 1996]

- Provisions described below enable the court when making an EPO to attach an exclusion requirement so a suspected abuser can be removed / kept away from the home in which child is living, or the surrounding area.

NB.   Ex-parte orders may offend against Article 6 and especially in attaching exclusion requirements where it may also be argued there is a potential breach of Article 1 Protocol 1 of the Convention (Right to Peaceful Enjoyment of Possessions), i.e. one's home.

- Where the court is satisfied that the threshold criteria for an EPO are satisfied and it makes such an order, the court may also include an exclusion requirement **if** the following conditions are satisfied:

    - There is reasonable cause to believe if the 'relevant person' is excluded from a dwelling-house in which the child lives, the child will not be likely to suffer significant harm either if s/he is not removed (ie. s.44(1)(a)(i)), or does not remain (ie. s.44(1)(a)(ii), or because enquiries as per s.44(1) (b) or (c) will cease to be frustrated

    - Another person living in same dwelling-house (parent or not) is able and willing to give to the child the care which it would be reasonable to give her/him and that person consents to the inclusion of the exclusion requirement.

NB. An argument could be made in respect of potential breaches of Article 8 and Article 1 Protocol 1 of the Convention, and the proportionality principle previously referred to is also relevant.

- An 'exclusion requirement' for the purposes of s.44A CA 1989 is any one or more of the following provisions:

  - Requiring the relevant person to leave a dwelling-house in which s/he is living with a child

  - Prohibiting the relevant person from entering a dwelling-house in which the child lives

  - Excluding the relevant person from a defined area in which a dwelling-house in which the child lives is situated [s.44A(5) CA 1989 as inserted by s.52 & Sch.6 FLA 1996]

Duration of Exclusion Requirement In Emergency Protection Order [s.44A(4) CA 1989 as inserted by s.52 & Sch. 6 FLA 1996]

- The court may provide that the exclusion requirement is to have effect for a shorter period than the other provisions of the order.

NB. There is no power to extend exclusion requirements beyond interim or EPO stage and if continuing protection is sought, an application must be made by person with whom the child living, for an injunction under s.100 or perhaps a Prohibited Steps Order.

Power of Arrest [s.44A(5) CA 1989 as inserted by s.52 & Sch.6 FLA 1996]

- The exclusion requirement may have a power of arrest attached to it [s.44A(5)].Where it does so, the court may provide that the power of arrest is to have effect for a shorter period than the exclusion requirement [s.44A(6) CA 1989 as inserted by s.52 & Sch.6 FLA 1996].

NB.   Any period specified for the purposes of ss. (4) or (6) may be extended by the court on one or more occasions on an application to vary or discharge the EPO [s.44A(7) CA 1989 as inserted by s.52 & Sch.7 FLA 1996].

- Where a power of arrest is attached to an exclusion requirement of an EPO, a constable may arrest without warrant any person whom s/he has reasonable grounds to believe to be in breach of the requirement[s.44A(8) CA 1989 as inserted by s.52 & Sch.6 FLA 1996].

- If while an EPO containing an exclusion requirement is in force, the applicant has removed the child from the dwelling-house from which the relevant person is excluded, to other accommodation for a continuous period of over 24 hours, the order shall cease to have effect in so far as it imposes the exclusion requirement [s.44A(10) CA 1989 as inserted by s.52 & Sch.6 FLA 1996].

Undertakings Relating To Emergency Protection Orders [s.44B CA 1989 as inserted by s.52 & Sch.6 FLA 1996]

- In any case where the court has power to include an exclusion requirement in an EPO, the court may accept an undertaking from the relevant person and in such cases no power of arrest may be attached [s.44B(1) & (2) CA 1989 as inserted by s.52 & Sch.6 FLA 1996].

- Such an undertaking:

  - Is enforceable as if it were an order of the court

  - Will cease to have effect if, whilst it is in force, the applicant has removed the child from the dwelling-house from which relevant person is excluded to other accommodation for a continuous period of more than 24 hours [s.44B(3) CA 1989 as inserted by s.52 & Sch.6 FLA 1996]

- On the application of a person who is not entitled to apply for the order to be discharged, but is a person to whom an exclusion requirement contained in the order applies, an EPO may be varied or discharged by the court in so far as it imposes the exclusion requirement [s.45(8A) CA 1989 as inserted by s.52 & Sch.6 FLA 1996].

- Where a power of arrest has been attached to an exclusion requirement of EPO the court may, on the application of any person entitled to apply for the discharge of the order so far as it imposes the exclusion requirement, vary or discharge the order in so far as it confers a power of arrest (regardless of whether any application has been made to vary or discharge any other provision of the order) [s.45(8B) CA 1989 as inserted by s.52 & Sch.6 FLA 1996].

Challenge of EPO

- 72 hours after the making of an EPO, an application for a discharge can be made by parent, person with parental responsibility, child or anyone with whom child living at time of EPO

NB.   *Restricting the right to apply until after the elapse of 72 hours may be a potential infringement of the rights contained in Article 6 (Right To A Fair Trial).*

    Reasonable contact is assumed between child and above parties and can only be restricted by court direction. A court may be asked for / may give directions to limit contact and/or about medical / psychiatric examinations.

    A child of 'sufficient understanding' or aged 16 or over may refuse examination.

Discovery [s.48 (1) CA 1989]

- If necessary, a court may direct someone to disclose to applicant for EPO the whereabouts of a child.

NB. *A statement or admission made in complying with a*
court direction to disclose a child's whereabouts is
not admissible in evidence against person or spouse
in proceedings other than perjury.

Entry / Search [s.48 (3) CA 1989]

- An EPO may include directions to enter and search (but not by force).

Warrant [s.48 (9) and (10) CA 1989]

- Where a court believes applicant has been / is likely to be refused access to child it may issue a warrant to police to assist, using if necessary, reasonable force.

NB. *Court can direct that police be accompanied by a*
doctor, nurse or health visitor.

Police Powers of Protection (P.P.O.P) [s46 CA 1989]

Grounds [s.46 (1)] CA 1989

- Police must have reasonable grounds to believe child would otherwise suffer 'significant harm'.

NB. *P.P.O.P. may arguably breach Article 8(1)(Right To*
Respect for Private and Family Life). Although
Article 8(2) qualifies this right, the public authority's
interference must be 'proportionate'.

Effect

- A P.P.O.P.:

  - Allows a police constable to remove and accommodate child, or

  - Ensure that s/he remains in current location

  - Does not give parental responsibility

  - Does allow police to do all that is reasonable

Duration [s.46 (6) CA 1989]

- Up to 72 hours.

Conditions

- Police must inform parent, local authority and child of steps taken [s.46 (3) and (4)], and

- Transfer her / him as soon as possible to local authority accommodation, though the responsibility for ongoing enquiries and any decision to release child from police protection remains with the police.

NB. *Police can also apply for an EPO to be made in favour of a local authority. If so, any time spent in police protection must be deducted from time on EPO.*

Recovery Order [s.50 CA 1989]

Applications

- Local authority, N.S.P.C.C. and police if child on EPO or C.O. (including interim C.O.).

- Police if subject of P.P.O.P.

Grounds

- Child is subject to Care Order, EPO or in police protection, has run away or is being kept away from a responsible person who should be caring for her / him, or is missing

Effect

- Directs responsible person to produce child or to inform of whereabouts.

- Authorises police to search (using reasonable force if necessary), and

- Allows removal of child by authorised person.

- If foster carers, private or voluntary homes have a certificate from Secretary of State they are exempt from law covering abduction of children.

Child Assessment Order (C.A.O.) [s.43 CA 1989]

Applications

- By local authority or N.S.P.C.C. [s.43 (1) CA 1989].

NB. Applicant must provide 7 days notice to persons listed in s.43(11) and a court can treat the application as if it were for an EPO[s.43(3) CA 1989].

Grounds [s.43 (1) CA 1989]

- Applicant must satisfy the court that s/he has reasonable cause to suspect child is suffering or is likely to suffer 'significant harm', and

  - Needs assessment of state of child's health or development or way in which s/he has been treated to determine if suffering or likely to suffer 'significant harm', and

  - Assessment is otherwise unlikely to be undertaken or to be satisfactory

NB. For a case where a local authority was reluctant to pay for a court ordered assessment but the House of Lords ordered it to proceed see Re C (Interim Care Order: Residential Assessment) [1997] 1 FLR 1.

Effect [s.43 (6) CA 1989]

- Obliges person/s to produce child and comply with court directions e.g. medicals and any other form of assessment – see Re C [1997] 1 FLR 1 [HL].

NB.   If of sufficient understanding or aged 16 or over, a child may refuse medical. If necessary, child may be kept from home.

Duration [s.43 (6) CA 1989]

- From a specified date and for such period, not exceeding seven days, which may be specified.

Rights of Refusal of Medical & Other Assessment [ss.38; 43; 44 CA 1989]

- The right of a child to refuse to submit to medical, psychiatric or dental investigations is limited to the assessment stages of the order provided for the above sections.

NB.   For the circumstances in which the child's refusal may be overruled, see South Glamorgan CC v W and B [1993] 1 FLR 574 where the High Court's inherent jurisdiction under s.100 CA 1989 was invoked to override the refusal of a 15 year old to psychiatric assessment in an interim Care Order s.38(6) direction.

Protection of Children Act 1999 (POCA 1999)

- The POCA 1999 requires 'regulated' child care organisations to check the names of anyone they propose to employ in posts involving regular contact with children, against both the:

  - DH 'Consultancy Service Index list' and
  - DfES 'List 99'

- A child care organisation is defined as an organisation:

  - Which is concerned with the provision of accommodation, social services or health services to children or the supervision of children
  - Whose activities are regulated by or by virtue of any prescribed enactment **and**
  - Which fulfils such other conditions as may be prescribed

- If a person is listed in either the DH or DfES indices, s/he may **not** (with some exceptions in the case of the DfES) be employed.

- The 'Disclosure Service' of the Criminal Records (CRB) provides two sorts of certificates of relevance to employers and one or other must be sought with respect to al candidates in relevant organisations who seek to work with children.

- A 'standard disclosure' is available for posts involving regular contact with children (and vulnerable adults), certain professions in health, law and pharmacy and indicates if there is nothing on record, or show details drawn from the police national computer of:

  - Spent and unspent convictions
  - Cautions, formal reprimands and warnings

- An 'enhanced disclosure' in addition the information provided by a standard disclosure may contain non-conviction information from local police records.

- The enhanced disclosure is available for posts involving regular caring for, training, supervision of or being in sole charge of children (or vulnerable adults).

- Both standard and enhanced disclosures will show whether a person is banned under s.4 Criminal Justice and Courts Act 2000 (CJCA 2000) from working or seeking work with under 18 year olds.

Partnership with Families

- Research has demonstrated the value of good relationships between families and professionals in bringing about optimum outcomes for children.

- *The Challenge of Partnership in Child Protection* (DH 1995) outlines the following basic principles for working in partnership:

  - Dignity and respect afforded the family

  - Family made aware that child's safety and welfare the first priority, though all members entitled to courteous and competent service

  - Minimising infringement of privacy consistent with welfare of the child

  - Clarity at all stages about powers and purpose of intervention

  - Remaining aware of the impact of professional intervention

  - Respecting confidentiality, passing on information only with permission or where necessary to protect a child

  - Listening to concerns of all family members and exploring their feelings and wishes before concluding professional explanations and plans

- Exploring children's place within family and community, including cultural and religious contexts

- Considering strengths and potential of family as well as weaknesses and limitations

- Ensuring children family and others know their responsibilities and rights and the consequences of accepting or refusing services

- Using plain, jargon-free language appropriate to age and culture of each person

- Being open and honest about concerns and responsibilities

- Allowing children and adults to absorb professional concerns and processes

- Distinguishing between personal values, feelings etc and professional roles and responsibilities and ensuring receipt of effective supervision

- Admitting and explaining any mistake or misinterpretation, acknowledging and working to minimise consequent distress to children and adults

- A child of sufficient capacity should be helped to understand how child protection processes work and how s/he can contribute to decisions about the future.

- The child should though be helped to accept that decisions will be taken in the light of all available information from professionals, parents and other family members as well as that which s/he provides.

Sensitivity to Race, Culture, Ethnicity, Religion & Preferred Language

- Children from all cultures may be abused or neglected.

- So as to make sensitive and informed professional judgements about a child's needs, professionals must be sensitive to differing family patterns, lifestyles and child rearing patterns which vary across racial, ethnic and cultural groups.

- Working in a multi-racial and multi-cultural society requires professionals and organisations to be committed to anti-discriminatory practice.

- Professionals must guard against positive or negative myths and stereotypes about black and other minority ethnic families.

- The focus of work must remain always on the needs of individual children.

- It is critical that families understand the child protection process and professionals must provide clear, accessible oral and written information (where necessary, in the family's preferred language).

Information Sharing & Confidentiality

- Research and experience indicates that to keep children safe professionals must share relevant information across geographical and professional boundaries.

- Information relevant to child protection will be about:

  - Health and development of a child and her/his exposure to possible harm

  - A parent / carer who is unable to care adequately for a child

  - Other individuals who may present a risk of harm to the child

- The duty of all professionals providing services to adults or to children, is to place the needs of the child first.

- Doctors, nurses and other health staff, teachers and social workers should be confident that their practice with respect to information sharing is both lawful and in accordance with required professional standards.

Relevant Law

- The main sources of relevant law with respect to information sharing and confidentiality are:

  - Common law

  - European Convention on Human Rights (introduced to UK law via the Human Rights Act 1998)

  - Data Protection Act 1998

  - The Caldicott Standards (which apply to health and social services)

  - Children Act 1989

- The *'Common Law Duty of Confidence'* requires that personal information about children and families kept by professionals and agencies, should not generally be disclosed without the consent of the subject.

- It is lawful to disclose such information if it appears necessary to do so to safeguard a child/ren in the public interest i.e. public interest in protecting children may override public interest in maintaining confidentiality.

- Disclosure must be justifiable in accordance with the facts of each case.

- *NB. If information is trivial or already in the public domain, there is no breach of confidence when it is shared e.g. a social worker who was concerned about a child's whereabouts might phone the school to establish if she/ was in school that day.*

The approach to confidential information should be the same whether the proposed disclosure is within one or between more than one agency.

- Article 8 of the European Convention on Human Rights states that:

  - Everyone has the right to respect for her/his private and family life, home and correspondence

  - There shall be no interference by a public authority with the exercise of this right except in accordance with the law and as is necessary in a democratic society in the interests of national security, public safety or economic well being of the country, for prevention of disorder or crime, for the protection of health or morals, or for the protection of the rights and freedoms of others

- Disclosure of information (appropriate for the purpose and only to the extent that is necessary) is justified if it is (as per the criteria in Article 8 above) to:

  - Safeguard a child

  - Protect her/his health or morals

  - Protect the rights and freedoms of others or

  - Prevent disorder or crime

- When disclosing information without consent, the extent of the disclosure must be 'proportionate' to the need, i.e. disclosure must be limited to that which is absolutely necessary to achieve the aim of the disclosure.

- The Data Protection Act 1998 (DPA 1998) requires that personal information is:

  - Obtained and processed fairly and lawfully

  - Processed for limited purposes and not in any manner incompatible with those purposes

  - Accurate and relevant

  - Held for no longer than necessary

  - Kept secure

  - Only disclosed in appropriate circumstances

- The DPA 1998 does allow disclosure of information, (without the subject's consent) for the purposes of, or where not so doing is likely to prejudice:

  - Prevention or detection of crime

  - Apprehension or prosecution of offenders

- *'Caldicott'* principles and processes offer a framework of quality standards for the management within health and local authorities of personal information.

- Health and social services must ensure that their information sharing practices are compliant with HSC/LAC 2002/003/LAC (2002) 2 'Implementing the Caldicott Standards Into Social Care'.

NB.   *Each health and social services organisation should have a named 'Caldicott guardian' who can provide advice.*

Professional Guidance for Doctors

- *Working Together to Safeguard Children* (1999) DH, refers to the General Medical Council (GMC) guidance entitled *Confidentiality: Protecting and Providing Information* (1995 and subsequently updated in 2000).

- The above guidance emphasises the importance in most circumstances of obtaining a patient's consent to the disclosure of personal information but makes clear that information may be released (without consent) to third parties e.g. statutory agencies such as social services and police, if:

    - A failure to disclose information may expose the patient, or others, to risk of death or serious harm.

- The GMC has confirmed that its guidance refers to information about:

    - Third parties who are of direct relevance to child protection, e.g. adults who may pose a risk to a child

    - Children who may be the subject of abuse

Professional Guidance for Nurses & Other Health Staff

- The United Kingdom Central Council for Nursing, Midwifery and Health Visiting (UKCC) - now renamed the Nursing and Midwifery Council (NMC) - produced *Guidelines for Professional Practice* (1996) containing the advice that disclosure of information may occur:

  - With the consent of the patient or client

  - Without the consent of the patient or client when disclosure is required by law or by court order

  - Without the consent of the patient or client when the disclosure is considered to be necessary in the public interest (public interest is defined to include child protection)

Professional Guidance for Police Services

- Police are lawfully able to supply information to relevant third parties for defined categories of request.

- Care must be taken to ensure all information disclosed is accurate, topical, factual, proportionate for the purpose for which it is passed and above all, relevant and necessary to the issue and the individual concerned

- The categories of request for information which police can lawfully respond to are those in which:

  - A child protection referral is made and a joint investigation under s.47 CA 1989 begun

- Information is requested as part of an inter-agency risk management meeting set up under the SOA 1997

- Social services are carrying out a s.47 CA 1989 enquiry on a single agency basis

- Social services are carrying out an initial assessment in order to inform a decision as to the justification for a s.47 enquiry

- Social services are carrying out a 'child in need' assessment under s.17 CA 1989

- The request relates to a child on the child protection register

- Social services is faced with immediate need to place a child with a family member or friend in an emergency

■ Information must be provided by the police on the strict understanding it is confidential in nature, will be used only for purposes of a child protection / in need assessments and may not be passed on to any third party without the express permission of the police.

Professional Guidance for Education Staff

■ Guidance from the then DfEE (Circular 10/95) indicated staff had a professional responsibility to share information about protection of children with other professionals, particularly police and social services.

■ New and more explicit obligations introduced by s.175 EA 2002 are laid out on pages 21 –25 above.

Professional Guidance for Social Workers

- The British Association of Social Workers (BASW) 2002 Code of Ethics allows for divulging confidential information without consent of the service user or informant when there is:

  - Clear evidence of serious danger to the service user, worker or other persons

Summary of Information Transfer Position

- All professionals may therefore share information without the consent of parents/carers only if:

  - Seeking permission might place the child at increased risk of significant harm or

  - Such action might reasonably assist in the prevention or detection of serious crime

Routine Agency Checks

- The consent of a parent or other person with parental responsibility must ordinarily be sought on those occasions when there is a need to gather further information via checks with other agencies, in order to:

  - Progress a s.17 assessment of need

  - Decide whether to re-designate a s.17 assessment of need to a s.47 enquiry or

  - Inform a s.47 enquiry

- Such checks may be completed without the above consents (in both s.17 and s.47 scenarios) if:

  - Seeking consent is believed likely to increase the perceived risk to the child/ren concerned or

  - A request for consent has been refused and sufficient professional concern remains to justify such action

Record Keeping

- Clear and accurate records are essential to effective multi-agency working and provide:

  - A documented account of individual and agency involvement

  - Continuity when an individual worker changes or is unavailable

  - A tool for managers to monitor or peers to review work

  - A source of information for enquiries

  - Evidence in case of a court hearing

- All agencies must have policies and arrangements for safe retention and prompt retrieval of records.

- Records must be clear and concise and differentiate between:

  - Fact

  - Opinion

- Judgements and
- Hypothesis

- It should be possible to track from the records kept (usually by social services):

  - The relevant history of the child / family which led to the intervention

  - The nature of interventions, including intended outcomes

  - Methods by which change is to be achieved and

  - Progress being made

NB.   Lord Laming's report included a number of recommendations for social services and health staff about effective record keeping.

Professional Supervision

- All those involved in child protection should have access to advice and support from peers, managers, named and designated professionals.

- Supervision should scrutinise and evaluate work and case records include key decisions reached during supervision.

Domestic Violence

- Prolonged and/or regular exposure to domestic violence can have a serious effect on the development and emotional well being of a child (including an unborn child whose mother may be kicked in her abdomen).

- In addition to assessing the impact on a child of observing domestic violence between adult partners, professionals should be alert to the strong link between domestic violence and child abuse.

NB. *The definition of 'harm' in s.31(9) CA 1989 will be extended by the ACA 2002 to include 'for example, impairment suffered from seeing or hearing the ill-treatment of another [s.120 ACA 2002].*

NB. *See the CAE companion guide 'Domestic Violence' which explains available legal remedies.*

Children with a Disability

- Available UK evidence suggests disabled children are at increased risk of abuse and neglect and presence of multiple disabilities appears to further increase the risk.

- Some may be at increased risk because they:

  - Have fewer outside contacts than other children

  - Receive intimate personal care, possibly from a number of carers

- Have impaired capacity to resist or avoid abuse

- Have communication difficulties which may make it difficult to tell others what is happening

- Are inhibited about complaining for fear of losing services

- Are especially vulnerable to bullying and intimidation by adults or peers

Children Living Away From Home

- A variety of safeguards can reduce risk of abuse / neglect in managed or contracted care settings, in secure units, YOIs and in prisons:

  - Children feeling valued and respected

  - An openness to the external world, including families and community

  - Staff / carers trained in all aspects of safeguarding children

  - Ready access by children to trusted adults

  - Clear, accessible and effective complaints procedures

  - Rigorous recruitment and selection procedures

  - Clear procedures and support systems for dealing with expressions of concern by staff / carers about their peers

  - A respect for diversity and sensitivity to race, religion, gender, sexuality and disability

- Effective supervision and support extending to temporary staff and volunteers

■ S.118 ACA 2002 when implemented, will require a local authority to appoint an independent reviewing officer to participate in and monitor effectiveness of reviews of looked after children. This officer can refer a case to an officer of the Children, Family Court Advisory and Support Service (CAFCASS) if s/he consider it appropriate to do so, and the CAFCASS officer will be empowered to apply to return the case to court.

NB. This provision introduces a review power similar to that argued for by the Court of Appeal in the starred milestones case Re S and RE W [2001] 2 FLR.

Prostitution

■ Children involved in prostitution and other forms of commercial sexual exploitation should be treated primarily as victims of abuse.

■ *'Safeguarding Children Involved in Prostitution'* DH 2000 offers guidance on the management of children / young people abused through prostitution.

Internet

■ Research indicates that a significant minority of those who access child pornography via the internet are also active abusers.

- When an individual is discovered to have accessed or placed child pornography on the internet, the police should be informed and his/her access to children should be established, both within the family and in employment and any other relevant settings.

NB. *In January 2003 the government announced an intention to include in the Sexual Offences Bill 2003 a new offence of 'grooming' a child via the internet.*

Mobile Families

- When families move (or are moved) frequently it is difficult to provide effective support or protection services.

- Aside from any other specific indicators that the child is suffering / may be suffering significant harm , the following features are often associated with mobile families within which a child is at risk:

  - Temporary or no registration with a GP

  - A child not on a school roll

  - Information 'patch-worked' across agencies with none holding a complete data set

  - A& E departments treating a child who is not linked into any local health services

- Collation and efficient sharing across agencies of accurate information about such families will assist in risk reduction.

Missing Children & Families

- Local agencies and professionals must consider, with respect to a child about whom there are concerns, that a series of missed appointments or abortive home visits may indicate that the family has suddenly move away.

- In the above circumstances, both social services and police must be notified and will need to initiate enquiries.

- Consideration may need to be given to legal action if it appears that a child for whom there are outstanding protection concerns, may be removed from the UK to avoid protection agencies.

Fabricated or Induced Illness

- This condition has also been described as:

  - Fabricated or induced illness by proxy

  - Factitious illness by proxy and

  - Munchausen's Syndrome by proxy

- The condition may be suggested when a parent (usually the mother) or carer of a small child:

  - Fabricates signs and symptoms including past medical history

  - Falsifies medical charts, records, letters and documents and specimens

  - Induces illness by a variety of means

- Harm to the child may be caused through unnecessary and invasive medical treatment based upon symptoms falsely described or deliberately manufactured by the parent / carer and not independently corroborated.

- *Safeguarding Children in Whom Illness is Fabricated or Induced* DH 2002 offers official guidance which supplements that provided in *Working Together to Safeguard Children DH 1999 / Welsh Assembly 2000.*

NB. *Note also the decision of the European Court in P C and S v UK [2002] 2 FLR 631 which laid down that the parents in such cases of Munchausen's syndrome must have their full Article 6 rights including the right to appropriate legal representation guaranteed by the courts in this country.*

Female Genital Mutilation (FGM)

- The Prohibition of Female Circumcision Act 1985 makes female circumcision, excision or infibulation an offence, except on specific health grounds.

- A local authority may need to invoke s.47 CA 1989 if it appears a child is likely to become the subject of FGM.

- In those areas which contain minority ethnic groups known to practice FGM, the ACPC policy should focus on a preventive strategy including community education.

Complex (Organised or Multiple) Child Abuse

- Organised or multiple abuse may be defined as abuse involving one or more abuser and a number of related or non-related abused children. The abusers may be acting in concert, in isolation or may be using an institutional framework or position of authority to recruit children.

- Guidance in *Working Together to Safeguard Children* has been supplemented as recommended by the Waterhouse enquiry report 'Lost in Care'.

- *Complex Child Abuse Investigations: Inter-Agency Issues* DH & HO May 2002 provides guidance about the special measures which may be required e.g. formation of dedicated strategic management and investigation teams.

Allegations Against Staff, Carers & Volunteers

- An allegation should be tested against the need for:
  - Criminal investigation
  - A child protection enquiry
  - Disciplinary or regulatory response or
  - Investigation as a complaint

- It is essential that all allegations are examined objectively by staff who are independent of the service, organisation or institution involved.

- ACPC agencies must, and other agencies providing services to children should have explicit procedures for handling allegations, which should be backed up by staff training and supervision.

- The common facts of alleged abuse must be applied independently to each of the possible response i.e. the fact that prosecution is not possible does not mean that action in relation to safeguarding children or employee discipline is not necessary or feasible.

- Parents of affected children should be given information about the concerns, advised of the processes being followed and results, so long as this does not impede the enquiry process itself.

NB. See page 24 for role of Investigation and Support Co-Ordinators with respect to allegations made against teachers.

Referral of a Child Believed to be At Risk

■ The child's immediate safety must be safeguarded and the law (s.3(5) CA 1989) allows anyone with actual care of a child e.g. a teacher or a health staff to 'do what is reasonable in all the circumstances of the case for the purpose of safeguarding or promoting a child's welfare'.

Referral Route

■ A referral should generally be made to the social services department covering the child's home address.

■ If the above information is unknown a referral should be made to the nearest social services department.

■ Maximum personal information about child, her/his circumstances and cause/s of concern should be relayed (but a referral must not be delayed to increase the available information).

■ The referrer should record in writing and sign the time, date and content of her/his discussions or contact with:

- Child
- Parent/s
- Agency manager and
- Social services

Involvement of Child

- Where abuse is alleged by a child, the response should be limited to listening carefully to what is said so as to:

  - Clarify the concerns

  - Offer re-assurance about how s/he will be kept safe and

  - Inform her/him what action will be taken

Involvement of Parent/s

- Where possible, concerns should be discussed with the family and agreement sought for a referral to social services unless it is concluded the process of discussing the concern may, by delay or the behavioural response it prompts, place the child at increased risk.

- A decision by any professional not to seek parental permission before making a referral to social services must be recorded and the reasons given (where a parent has agreed to a referral, this must be recorded and confirmed in the referral to social services).

Social Services Response to a Referral

- Social services, having considered the information provided, the views of other key agencies and any existing records, may determine there needs to be:

  - No further action

  - An 'initial' or 'core' assessment of need (with or without provision of a service)

  - A s.47 enquiry and/or emergency protective action

Initial & Core Assessments

- An 'initial assessment of need' as described in the *'Framework for the Assessment of Children In Need and Their Families'* DH 2000 must be completed within 7 working days.

- A professional referrer should ordinarily be informed of the outcome of such an initial assessment

- A 'core assessment' (which must be completed within 35 working days) may be justified:

  - As a result of an initial assessment

  - When a strategy discussion / meeting agrees it

  - When new information about an open case indicates that its is required

NB. *In the case of R On the Application of AB and SB v*
Nottingham City Council [2001] 3 FCR 350, the
court found that where a local authority used an
approach other than the 'core assessment', it was
obliged to adopt a similarly systematic one which into
account the domains of the child's developmental
needs, parents' capacity and family and
environmental factors. Failure to collaborate with all
relevant agencies so as to identify the child's needs,
produce a care plan and provide the identified
services would (without good cause) be unlawful.

Immediate Protection

- Where there is a risk to the life of a child or a likelihood of serious immediate harm, rapid action will be required and the duties and powers available to police and social services are described on pages 33-48.

- The local authority in which the child is found is responsible for initiating any emergency action.

Strategy Discussion / Meeting

- Whenever there is reasonable cause to suspect that a child is suffering or likely to suffer significant harm, there should be a strategy discussion involving social services, police and other agencies as appropriate, in particular any referring agency.

- The purposes of a strategy discussion are to:

  - Share available information

- Decide whether s.47 enquiries should be initiated or continued if already in motion

- Plan how enquiries should be handled

- Agree what immediate action is needed to ensure the child's safety and/or offer services or support

- Determine what information about the discussion will be shared with the family (unless such information sharing may place a child at risk of significant harm or jeopardise police investigations into any alleged offence)

Conduct of s.47 Enquiries

- Enquiries may be conducted by social services or police alone or jointly.

- Each ACPC should have a protocol to guide both agencies in deciding how s.47 enquiries and associated police investigations should be conducted (reinforced by Lord Laming's report).

- *The Framework for the Assessment of Children in Need and Their Families* DH 2000 provides a structure for collection and analysis of information gathered in the course of a s.47 enquiry, which the courts have now determined must be followed (see R on the application of AB and SB v Nottingham City Council cited above).

- Those with parental responsibility for a child must be informed at the earliest possible opportunity of s.47

enquiries unless doing so would jeopardise safety of this or any other child or undermine a criminal investigation.

■ All children within a household should be seen during the course of an enquiry and those who are the focus of the enquiry should (subject to age and generally with parental consent) be seen alone.

Evidential Video Interviews

■ Joint video interviews involving police and social services may proceed if **all** the criteria in part 1 below and **any** of those in part 2 are met:

Part 1

- Child is under eighteen years old

- Child is able or can be facilitated to provide a clear account and

- It is clearly in her/his interests to proceed

Part 2

- Direct statement by a child of sexual abuse made to a chosen adult or another child

- Confession by a person about sexual abuse or serious assault on named child

- Direct statement by a child of serious physical abuse

- Paediatrician's opinion that the child has experienced sexual abuse or has a serious injury/condition where there are concerns as to its cause

- Child is a witness to a grave or serious crime

■ A video interview will be inappropriate if a child's religion forbids it or if s/he has no expressive language.

■ Subject to the child's informed consent (or a parent if the child is judged too young to provide it) a video interview may proceed and must be conducted by suitably trained staff in manner consistent with the guidance contained in *Achieving Best Evidence in Criminal Proceedings* HO 2002

Outcome of Enquiries

■ Following a single agency or joint investigation, the concerns may be:

- Unsubstantiated
- Substantiated though assessed as posing no ongoing risk of significant harm or
- Substantiated and posing a continuing risk of significant harm

■ In the latter case, the core assessment must be completed and an 'initial child protection conference 'convened.

■ The maximum time which may elapse from a decision to initiate a s.47 enquiry and an initial conference is 15 working days.

Initial Conference

- An initial child protection conference must be convened no later than 15 working days following the (or last of the) strategy discussion/s.

- Purposes of strategy meetings (which bring together family members, child (when appropriate), supporters / advocates and involved professionals) are to:

  - Collate and analyse in an inter-agency setting the information gathered about a child's health, development and functioning, parent/s' capacity to ensure the child's safety and promote her/his health and development

  - Make judgements about the likelihood of a child suffering significant harm in the future and whether there are sufficient concerns to place the child on the protection register

  - Decide what future action is needed to safeguard the child and promote her/his welfare, how that action will be taken forward and with what intended outcomes

  - Allocate a key worker for children placed on the protection register

  - Identify a multi-agency core group to develop and monitor the outline child protection plan

NB.   Failure to involve the family properly in such a meeting may result in an action for breach of human rights under Articles 6 and 8 see e.g. R v UK [1988] 2

FLR 445; and the decision of the Court of Appeal in
Re S and Re W [2001] 2 FLR 582 , which was
untouched on these points in relation to the possibility
of actions based on human rights claims. Also see Re
M (Care : Challenging Decisions by Local Authority)
[2001] 2 FLR 1300 where the local authority had
reached decisions about the child in a crisis meeting
which the parents did not attend because they did not
know it was being held, which was deemed by the
court to be a breach of Article 8..

Registration

- The decision to register a child must take account of the views of all agencies represented at the conference and will normally be consensual.

- Where agreement cannot be reached about registration, the decision falls to the conference chairperson.

- Any dissent must be recorded in the minutes of the conference

Pre-Birth Conference

- A pre-birth initial conference may be held when there is a need to consider whether (usually following a pre-birth assessment) an inter-agency protection plan is required.

- A pre-birth conference should be held:

  - Where an assessment gives rise to concerns that an unborn child may be at risk of significant harm

- A previous child has died or been removed from parent/s as a result of significant harm

- Where a child is to be born into a household which already has a child/ren on the child protection register

- A schedule 1 offender lives in the household or is known to be a regular visitor

Review Conference

- The purposes of review conferences (first of which must be held within 3 months of the initial conference and thereafter at intervals of not more than 6 months) are to:

  - Evaluate the safety, health and development of the child with respect to the intended outcomes set out in the child protection plan

  - Ensure protective measures adopted are effective

  - Assess the likelihood of future significant harm and agree action accordingly, including the justification for continuing registration

Complaints About Conferences

- Parents, carers or a child (considered by chairperson to have sufficient understanding) may make a complaint in respect of one of the following aspects of conferences:

  - Process employed

  - Outcome, in terms of fact of and/or category of initial or continuing registration

- Decision not to register, to de-register or to continue registration

- The complaints process cannot itself change a registration decision and the end result for the complainant will be either that:

  - A conference is re-convened under a different chairperson

  - A review conference is brought forward or

  - It confirms the conclusions of the original conference

- Annexe B of LASSL(2001)02 provides statutory guidance on how to manage complaints and replaced paragraphs 5.71 to 5.73 of *Working Together to Safeguard Children.*

NB. See also for the possibility of an allegation of a breach of human rights Re M(Care : Challenging decisions by Local Authority [2001] 2 FLR 1300.

- S.117(2) ACA 2002 when implemented, will extend the scope of the s.26 CA 1989 complaints and representations procedure to include Parts IV and V of that Act (care and supervision and protection of children respectively) as well as adoption services. Regulations yet to be produced will detail these new provisions.

NB. S.119 ACA 2002 will make it obligatory for local authorities to offer an advocacy service to children and young persons who wish to make a formal complaint.

Appendix 1: Consent & Refusal of Medical Assessment or Treatment

General Principles

- The consent (of a parent with parental responsibility, patient her/himself or of a court) is a necessary prerequisite for treatment of all under eighteen year olds.

NB. The effect of consent is to protect the practitioner from a claim in trespass / charge of assault.

- In an emergency a doctor is lawfully entitled to undertake such treatment as appears necessary to safeguard the life and health of a patient until such time as consent can be sought from one of the above sources.

Consent of a Competent Minor of 16 or 17 Years of Age

- A minor of 16 or 17 has a specific right to give consent to surgical, medical or dental treatment [s.8 FLRA 1969].

- Unless grounds exist for believing that s/he might be mentally incompetent within the meaning of the MHA 1983 no further consent is required.

NB. This right does not extend to the donation of blood or organs.

- A person who has parental responsibility for a young person of this age cannot override her/his consent (cf.-refusal below).

Consent by a Competent Minor of Less than 16 Years of Age

- A child (of any age) who has 'sufficient understanding to make an informed decision' is able to give a valid consent to treatment.

- A judgement as to the child's level of understanding would normally be for the doctor (in consultation with others as necessary) to form, and the degree of understanding needed would of course be greater, the more complicated the treatment.

NB.   The consent of an under sixteen year old who has sufficient understanding cannot be overridden by a person with parental responsibility.

Refusal of Treatment by a Minor of Any Age

- The Court of Appeal has expressed the view that a consent from someone who has parental responsibility would legitimise treatment of an unwilling minor of sixteen or seventeen, or an under sixteen year old of 'sufficient understanding'.

NB.   The consent of only one person who has parental responsibility is required.

Refusal by Persons with Parental Responsibility and a Competent Minor

- Where those with parental responsibility and a competent child are not prepared to give consent it would be necessary to invoke the inherent jurisdiction of the High Court so it could provide the necessary consent.

- Where the local authority has parental responsibility by virtue of a Care or interim Care Order, it could provide consent to proposed medical treatment.

- If, parent/s or others with parental responsibility were unwilling to consent, the local authority would be obliged to seek a court order to authorise it [South Glamorgan County Council v A & B 1993 2 FLR].

Refusal by Those with Parental Responsibility of Treatment for a Child Not considered 'Competent'

- If there is no one with parental responsibility who is prepared to give the necessary consent and the child is not considered competent, an application can be made to:

  - A court for a Specific Issue Order

  - The High Court to exercise its inherent jurisdiction to grant leave to administer the proposed treatment

- The court's decision will override any objection by the child or others with parental responsibility.

- If there is insufficient time to make such an application Ministry of Health guidance F/P9/1B and Home Office Circular 63/1968 should be followed.

- These suggest that a consultant may give treatment if s/he has had a full discussion with parents, obtained written support from a colleague to the effect that the child's life is in danger if treatment is withheld and an acknowledgement from the parents that in spite of the risk, they are still refusing their consent.

- Also as a matter of common law, where a doctor decides in an emergency to take any necessary steps to save the life of a child, it is not possible to take any legal action against her/him arising from that decision (unless s/he can be shown to have been negligent).

Specific Rights of Child To Refuse Assessment or Treatment

- The Children Act 1989 in theory, provides that a child who is subject to the following Orders and who has 'sufficient understanding to make an informed decision' has a specific right to refuse medical or psychiatric examination or any other form of assessment:

  - Interim Supervision or interim Care Order [s.38(6) CA 1989]

  - Child Assessment Order [s.43(8) CA 1989]

- Emergency Protection Order [s.44(7) CA 1989]
- Supervision Order [Sch.3 Para.4 CA 1989]

■ It has now been made clear in a series of cases that such refusals can be overridden by an Order of the High Court using its inherent jurisdiction [South Glamorgan County Council v A & B 2 FLR 1993].

■ In the case of interim Supervision and interim Care Orders, Child Assessment Orders and Emergency Protection Orders, the judgement of 'sufficient understanding' is for professional determination.

■ In the case of directions imposed within a full Supervision Order, it is for the court to determine. However, even a competent child's refusal can be overruled as described above.

Appendix 2: Confidentiality & Contraception

- All doctors' patients (including those aged less than sixteen) have a general right to confidentiality.

- In very rare cases e.g. if a doctor believes that a young person is being abused/exploited and is unable to persuade that young person to permit confidentiality to be relaxed, s/he should tell the young person of her/his intentions and inform the relevant agencies.

- A doctor is entitled to give contraceptive advice or treatment to those of less than sixteen **if**:

  - The young person understands the doctor's advice

  - The doctor cannot persuade the young person to inform her/his parent/s or allow the doctor to do so

  - The young person is very likely to begin or continue having intercourse with or without contraceptive treatment

  - The young person's physical and/or mental health are likely to suffer without advice/treatment

  - The young person's best interests require the doctor to give advice and/or treatment without parental consent

NB.   The above criteria are known as the Fraser guidelines.

■ Where a doctor decides **not** to respond to a young person's request, s/he does not have to inform parent/s.

■ The doctor should encourage the young person to inform, or allow the doctor to inform, the parent/s.

■ In the case of a young person, subject of a Care Order to a local authority, parental responsibility is shared by that local authority with the young person's parent/s.

■ If such a young person does not satisfy all the Fraser Guidelines criteria listed above (which would legitimise accepting the young person's consent only), then lawful consent can be provided by either a parent who has parental responsibility or the relevant local authority.

■ Unless to do so would place the young person at risk from the parent/s, the local authority which is told that such a young person is receiving contraceptive advice and/or treatment would usually inform the them.

Appendix 3: Source Documents

- The Challenge of Partnership in Child Protection DH 1995

- Working Together to Safeguard Children (England): DH et al 1999 Welsh Assembly 2000

- Safeguarding Children Involved in Prostitution – Supplementary Guidance to Working Together DH et al 2000 *www.doh.gov.uk/quality.htm*

- National Plan For Safeguarding Children From Commercial Sexual Exploitation *www.doh.gov.uk/qualityprotects*

- Framework for the Assessment of Children in Need & Their Families DH 2000

- Achieving Best Evidence in Criminal Proceedings HO 2001

- Reference Guide To Consent for Examination or Treatment DH 2001 *www.doh.gov.uk/consent*

- LASSL (2001) 02 The Children and Family Courts Advisory and Support Service (CAFCASS) and Complaints About the Functioning of Child Protection Conferences

- Safeguarding Children in Whom Illness Is Fabricated or Induced DH 2002

- Complex Child Abuse Investigations: Inter-Agency Issues DH & HO May 2002

- Learning from Past Experience – A Review of Serious Case Reviews DH June 2002

- Lord Laming's Report of the Inquiry Into the Death of Victoria Climbie DH 2003 *www.victoria-climbie-inquiry.org.uk/report*

- London Child Protection Procedures (edition 1) 2003 drafted on behalf of the London Child Protection Committee by Edi Carmi and Fergus Smith

- Child Abuse (3rd edition) Christina Lyon et al, Family Law 2003 ISBN 0-85308-576-5

- Young People Facing Forced Marriages – Guidelines for Social Workers (consultation version DH 2003)

- Draft version of National Guidance to be circulated to relevant agencies in May 2003 via DH / DfES / HO

- All relevant legislation

Appendix 4: CAE Publications

- Personal Guides:

  - Children Act 1989 in the Context of the Human Rights Act 1998

  - Childminding and Day Care (England)

  - Child Protection

  - Residential Care of Children

  - 'How Old Do I Have To Be ?' (a simple guide to the rights and responsibilities of 0 - 21 year olds)

  - Adoption Act 1976

  - Domestic Violence - (Part IV Family Law Act 1996 & Protection from Harassment Act 1997)

  - Human Fertilisation and Embryology Act 1990

  - Looking After Children: Good Parenting, Good Outcomes (DH LAC System)

  - Crime and Disorder Act 1998 in the Context of the Powers of Criminal Courts (Sentencing) Act 2000

Available from: 103 Mayfield Road South Croydon Surrey CR2 0BH   tel:020 8651 0554   fax:020 8405 8483
email: childact@dial.plpex.com

www.caeuk.org

Discounts for orders of 100 or more of any one title